Potholes
in the
Universe

"We are as a splinter in God's thumb,
a link lost in love's synchronicity with life.
We are become the despoilers of paradise,
potholes in an otherwise perfect universe."

by Frederick Michaels

Potholes

in the

Universe

The Poetry of
Frederick Michaels

Robin A. Rothman, Editor

Chatter House Press
Indianapolis, Indiana

Potholes
in the
Universe

For information:

Chatter House Press
7915 S Emerson Ave, Ste B303
Indianapolis, IN 46237

chatterhousepress.com

ISBN: 978-1-937793-35-7
Library of Congress Control Number: 2016941814

DEDICATION

This collection of poems is dedicated to my loving and inspiring wife, Penny and the equally loving, important women in my life — Robin, Penny, Taran and Kelsey. You are the rhythm in my verse and the rhyme in my soul.

ACKNOWLEDGEMENT

I would like to sincerely thank my daughter Robin for the many hours she spent editing this book. Sometimes the truth might be right before your eyes, but "hidden in your tall weeds of self doubt" and obscured by poor punctuation.

The following poems have been published previously, sometimes in different forms. I am truly grateful to the publishers.

"Dahlia Waits", "Gettysburg in Winter", "Sitting at the Edge of the World", "In a Wheat Field", "Wars Are Fought By The Sons" and "The Gingerbread Man" appeared in *Reckless Writing* (Chatter House Press, 2012)

"Empathy In a Desecrated Cemetery" and "Where Have You Gone, Art Garfunkel?" appeared in *Reckless Writing 2013* (Chatter House Press, 2013)

"A Visit to Mounds State Park" and "McCormick's Creek State Park" appeared in *Naturally Yours*, (2013)

"Sing It Buffy Sainte-Marie" and "Lorraine" appeared in *Flying Island Literary Journal* (On-Line)

"Dying With Scott in Antarctica" appeared in the *Boston Poetry Journal* (On Line)

"One Last Dream" and "Reflections on The Pentagon Memorial" *Lone Stars Magazine* (San Antonio, TX)

An Assemblage of Poems

I. *Manifest Destiny*
Dahlia Waits   3
Promised Land   4
Darkness in All Of Us   5
Visions of an Old Graveyard   6
A Scene From The West   7
Tribal Woman at the Eiteljorg   8
Little Big Horn   9
Sing It Buffy Sainte-Marie   10

II. *Doorways to the Soul*
Once Candle Wick is Gone   13
In A Wheat Field   14
Holes   15
My Mom's Last Year   16
Keepsakes   18
Where Have You Gone, Art Garfunkel?   19
A Touch of the Past   20
The Gingerbread Man   21

III. *Santayana Sleeps*
Lorraine   25
Ukraine   26
Reflections on The Pentagon Memorial   27
Ruining What We Touch   28
Iraq Again   30
A Far, Far Better Thing Not Done   31
Freedom Dies A Little   32
Empathy in a Desecrated Cemetery   33

IV. Hearts Lost and Found

Teach Me Your Words   37
The Night Watchman   38
Four Haiku for You   39
Ode to Pat Benetar   40
Mourning Identity   41
Could   42
Betrothal   43
Love is Creative Destruction   44
Fear to Love   45
Choices   46
Not Just Passing Through   47
There Are Words   48

V. A Tour of Senses

Hay Baling   53
Whisperer   54
Dawn   55
Stars   56
In The City By The Bay   57
I Think I Went To Times Square Once   58
Cloud Farming   60
From My Kitchen Window   62
Seasonality   63
Overcast   64

VI. The Isle of Whimsy

Scooter The Cat   67
Piano Man   68
Daydream in Paradise   69
i-Man   70
Musings of an Idle Mind   71
A Slow Day At Starbucks   72
Weeds and Grass   74
Oh Furtzil Sweet Amines   75
A Warrior's Tale   76
Ever Been   77

VII. *Portraits and Portrayals*

Sitting on Death Row 81
Dregs Need Not Be Sour 82
Lincoln 83
Outliving 84
50 to Life 85
Oxford Literati 86
Pompeii and Herculaneum Unearthed 88
A Look Ahead 20 Years 89
Even the Dead Deserve A Song 90
One Last Dream 91

VIII. *God and Nature*

Sit at the Edge of the World 95
He's My God Too! 96
Dreams 98
Who Are We To Blame 99
Sandy 100
And God Said 101
McCormick's Creek State Park 102
A Visit to Mound State Park 104
Death on the Savanna 105
A Tanka to Buddha in the Cemetery 106

IX. *Words, Rhymes and Punctuation, Or Not*

Guilty of Poetry in the 3rd Degree 109
The View From City Lights 110
Coffee House Homage 111
Birthing a Poem 112
Poetry Before Breakfast 113
My Words at Rest 114
Peaches and Poetry 115
Special Refuge 116
Inside the Poet's Head 117
Muse 118

X. To Keep and Bear Arms

A Letter Found in the Trenches	121
Gettysburg in Winter	122
The Good Example	124
Wars Are Fought By The Sons	126
Dying With Scott In Antarctica	128
Walking With Pickett	130
On Cemetery Ridge	132
Standing in the WWII Memorial	133
Dying on Corregidor	134

I. Manifest Destiny

Dahlia Waits

Dahlia waits.
She stands aside the wooden chair.
Its hard frame wounds her body, yet
arisen, her pain is somewhat eased.
She stares from the painted post
out across the ancient desert landscape,
at scrub pines and sage; on Indian land.
Her land, won and lost so many years ago:
her mountains, thrust up like the earth's fist;
her hills, arroyos, canyons, streams, valleys.
"It's sterling silver, with fine turquoise."

She fashions fine jewelry for the tourists:
silver and semi-precious local stones,
white buffalo, onyx and hematite earrings.
It pays her way in a world she did not make,
a world she did not want — our world.
Dahlia waits,
for the old days and the old ways,
but they have been taken — without pity.
"Genuine Navajo hand-crafted jewelry."

Promised Land

They came from every distant corner
wearing scars of escaped oppression,
of cruel servitude or repressed spirit.
Eyes bright with perceived freedom,
a chance to build a new future, they
pooled at the old Mississippi like water,
ready to flood the western landscape
with an unstoppable tide of humanity.

Stand at the general store's window,
close aside that old muddy river road,
and watch the endless line of wagons.
Hear those painful wooden groans
sing from fully laden Conestogas, white
prairie schooners and tool-heavy freights.
They pass in slow review to the ferry,
on a nation's march to the promised land.

Darkness in All Of Us

How pitiless morning's glow of light
to end the night
and find the blood of slaughtered dreams
so strewn about the acrid ground,
as all around
the wolves' howls mimic echoed screams.

What conscience has such calloused heart
as plays a part
in madness that destroys a race
or tribe or single human soul,
no evil goal
or sign of evil men but commonplace?

We think our pages cleaner now
that blood somehow
has washed away across the years,
and what we were we will not be.
I hope that we
will not live down to greet our fears,

and see again the world in tears
no longer men, but cogs and gears.

Visions of an Old Graveyard

They tore the one church down right after the fire,
to hold children safe from the harm in its ruins.
Its well-mortared shell home to finches and starlings,
who now pick at bricks laying everywhere strewn.
No visitors come to its weedy old graveyard.
Its years are disguised in a patch overgrown.
The soil tillers packed up their plows after drought came;
gone searching for water and depths of black loam.

But many old stories in here lay abandoned,
asleep in the shade of this crop of carved stone:
some the mothers and fathers of this very nation
who conquered the land and then made it a home.
Both old and the young (different paths unto heaven),
the good with the bad (some devout and some not) —
all were somebody's someone, an epitaph written
in a family album, lost to where, we forgot.

Use fingers to trace out the names and the dating.
Feel the pioneer spirit that flows from the ground.
There are Ingalls and Crocketts, Boones, Natty Bumppo:
America's vanguard in the push westward bound.
I grieve at the state to which they've been forsaken —
no hint of remembrance, their grounds in decline.
If no one takes care to ensure they're respected
who'll step up for us in two hundred years' time?

A Scene From The West

Inspired by a painting in the
Eiteljorg Museum, Indianapolis, Indiana

Cold, white frosting greets dawn
beneath the mountain high,
dressing firs in bright fantasy
and urging cactus flowers to hide.
Glistening in western sunshine,
red velvet and vanilla sandstone
mimics half devoured layer cake,
abandoned by a mother nature
having apparently eaten her fill.
Only a faint aroma of breakfast
still lingering over our camp site
says anything of our being here.
When we've left, new fallen snow
will hopefully mask this as well.
We are on the run from the law
and they have Apache trackers.

Tribal Woman at the Eiteljorg

The lines on her face reveal wisdom
that is only gained with age and pain.
Yet, her smile speaks to a joy of giving,
of a world she has bettered in her time.
She, dressed of buckskin plains deer,
vouches for the culture of all the tribes,
from shore to shore in a homeland lost,
yet still tethered to the earth and wind.
Feel her take you into her painted heart.
She is as a tree grown into the landscape,
a weeping form flowing down to ground,
depicted today only in sepia photographs,
but alive in the very souls of her progeny.

Little Big Horn

Fractured and unsettling,
tense sound wraps echoes
around the bare grass hills,
darts along carved coulees,
fills a gray Montana sky.
It falls upon helpless ears
as plaintive cry, dying wail,
leaving no doubt to finality
of the horrors playing out
beyond Big Horn's horizon.

Blind vanity and stupidity —
drivers to life's final scene,
rife with dramatic futility.
History now rings down end
to legendary careers, but
also to tribal preeminence
on a continent of Iroquois,
Cherokee, Lakota, Apache.
Defended, a land they owned,
and now, could never keep.

Sing It Buffy Sainte-Marie

Crimson flesh and onyx flies —
a vicious scar across the plains.
Breath stealing rotted air
chokes off slaughtered vision.

Wagons heaped of black hides
snake away in morning haze
to rail heads and all points east,
into seamstresses' tiny hands.

Feathered men with teared eyes
knew the truth foretold by stars —
bloody knives will change lives,
gone nature's gift of food, clothes.

Arisen such time unwilled, lament
dead bison naked to your gaze.
Now governments become beasts,
a whole world — land despoiled.

II. Doorways to the Soul

Once Candle Wick is Gone

I am asleep, or should be,
for it is the hour set —
past both lullabies and kisses,
by my fears and all regret.
I can see your face so clearly
(it's the same as when we met),
still so calm and unrevealing
but, with cheeks so slightly wet.

The coat of fog you're wearing
spreads the light to make you glow;
so unlike your facial clarity
the rest is hard to know.
Be there one of you or many?
Are they standing by also
those who bred me? Ones I loved?
Yes, I truly hope it's so.

Can this dream be yet a vision
come to me from far beyond?
Pray tell, where burning flame hies
once the candle wick is gone?
Are you just a recollection, or
such flame as dances on?
Either warmth that so enfolds me
yields me peace to rest upon.

In A Wheat Field

An endless pale blue sky,
crushes the plane to the horizon.
Featureless, frozen miles of wheat
erect against the absence of wind,
are as if painted upon a canvas
without curves or angles.
It is a golden blanket
glinting in the sun.

If I lie down to sleep,
snug 'neath a warm wheat cover,
would vivid dreams of wife and home
renew my strength to journey on
or bid me stay and slumber?
Against my aching joints,
I set my tired feet
afoot upon the path.

Holes

there are holes in the yard
washed out by rain
dug out by rabbits
pitfalls for the unwary

awaiting a misplaced step
like a misspoken phrase

like holes in a roof
or holes in a life
not appearing overnight
but having steadily worn

through the grass
through the shingles

through the fine fabric
that is family and friendship
that is love and fondness
that is faith and forgiveness

you can patch sod with soil
you can patch a roof with pitch

My Mom's Last Year

There were brown edges to her,
youth and vigor having worn thin.
Yet, her smile could light the dark
as bright as a street lamp ablaze.
Her wit could bring a room alive
with infectious mirth and gaiety.

Recall a round but fragile voice,
pure joy gift wrapped in a song
when moods were light and airy,
quiet yet firm in earnest solemnity
when choice of words never failed,
being measured ever so precisely.

She preferred cherished memories
of old days over those more recent,
never missing the quaintest details,
recalled with a passion and pride
so typical of mothers only visited
when guilt quotients are exceeded.

During that last year, I called daily,
playing the role of the good son.
In truth, I reveled in her sounds,
desperate to untie the hard knot
of under-appreciated parentage,
tightened by my years of apathy.

But as a candle flickers at its end,
frailty overtakes the still warm glow.
Wick topples, flame is quenched.
Thus she left, yearning to join him
whose love was hers for so long,
her voice alive only in my memory.

Keepsakes

I keep my tomorrows
in a window box
where they can grow
with my dreams.

I keep today
on a shopping list
so I don't forget
to live my life.

I keep my yesterdays
in a memory book
so I can cherish

how lucky I've been.

Where Have You Gone, Art Garfunkel?

The heat hits you in the face like a brick
each time you roll down that window.
So you stick to the night air for toking,
freezing your ass off in the high desert.
Your Buick hums along to a six string
effortlessly finger-picked by Paul Simon,
and tires hug the empty road's centerline
like a needle in the groove of a vinyl LP.

Could have been your "goin' home" story,
'cept you ain't never been out here before.
Pretty odd being road cherry at your age,
and a bit late for that mid-life crisis crap.
Mighta been a down shift on life's last hill —
some extra torque to help pick up speed
as you made for that unwelcome finish line.
But then you got it, and now it's open road.

Don'tcha feel clean out on the highway,
freed of civilization and it's dirty hands?
Miles and miles of unprepackaged world
with prehistoric simplicity and stark beauty.
No contaminating baggage in the trunk
to drag thoughts back to that other scene.
Just a wad of cash, and no credit cards —
your signature's all zeroes now, man.

Sun's up, and you've lost your shades.
So you figure to keep on heading west,
maybe go somewhere they can't find you,
bump into Garfunkel. Where'd he go?

A Touch of the Past

There were holes in the wall
where pictures used to be.
I filled them with spackle
and painted over,
but left the memories.

It still has warts and scars;
fallout from family frolic.
I replastered damage
and sanded down,
yet still can feel the laughter.

It doesn't matter
the paint's mismatched,
or the surface isn't smooth.
This wall is my life.

It doesn't matter if you can't tell.
I see and hear it,
though the joy of it is only mine.

The Gingerbread Man

Where has gone the gingerbread man
who enfolded you deftly in his arms? And
what has befallen your teddy bear Paul?
Does his squeaky voice not still enthrall?

Oh, you've put away your foolish toys
and found new interest in handsome boys?
Does true love rise and spark your fires
for the particular one your heart desires?

And so you're bound, the seed's been sown
to have that family of your own,
to love and nurture and lives enfold —
indescribable pleasure as they grow old.

Now from your memory's recess find,
as your older days fill up with time,
the gingerbread man's come home again.
And so has teddy bear Paul, your friend.

III. Santayana Sleeps

Lorraine

Sweat rolls off the bridge of my nose.
I can taste a salty Main Street flavor
as I catch its 90° on my tongue tip
and share the brief liquidity with my lips.

It's just 25 minutes to the Lorraine,
but it surely feels like a long, hot way
from 1968 and the news on the TV.
I heard it plain then, but didn't feel it.

Comfortably unafflicted by deprivation,
cul du sac'd with like-minded faces,
insulated by middle class tunnel vision,
I was still numb and dumb from JFK in '63.

Now half a lifetime gone, the images
from my grainy black and white memory,
emotionless and a million miles removed,
snap into focus and I see all at once:

I am the hands on the rifle
I am the blood on the balcony
I am America unseen
behind a veil of indifference.

And as I peer through my view finder
I wonder how we do that to one another.
I wonder how we survive as men
and a bead of water drips down my lens.

Ukraine

the silence of peace
dies in city streets
like shattered glass
strewn on bloody cobblestones

fractured bones and hopes
ground up with mortar
for making barricades
now mausoleums for the dead

barely brave chest thumpers
pale bleeding hearts
bankrupt of honesty
yet righteous men of inaction

bellow too little too late
in endless diplomacy
frittering away time
to stand for our civilized society

a precious treasury of freedom
not meekly forfeit
to martial trumpets
but to feckless and feeble words

when those trumpets
were as yet still

Reflections on The Pentagon Memorial

An incredible weight of silence
pushes away the street noise,
and empties the ears of all but
the sound of our own breathing,
already muted by our fear
of disturbing its solemn peace.

We stand at the fanning of lines;
rays of years, focused upon a wall
where the granite doesn't match.
The lines are adorned with benches,
trees and sheltered reflecting pools.
We have no doubt they'd be pleased.

The tragedy still haunts this place,
making us look over our shoulders,
swearing we can hear the engines' whine;
but it's only the ever present wind,
pushing through the 184 maple trees,
gently calling us to remembrance.

And we will remember every detail,
humbled by the sheer elegance of it,
appalled by the terrible reason it exists,
yet somehow reassured by our people
so honoring the value of human lives
in a world where life... can be a weapon.

Ruining What We Touch

Both ancient Greeks and Romans knew
preeminence in their time,
but failed to learn what still is true:
that all must fall who climb.

We common men who earn our due
— our shoulders turn the wheel.
The payer and the planner, too
can profit from the deal.

A push, a nudge, an upward lift
gives all who need a start, and
just in kindness we do gift
ill-fortuned from our hearts.

Yet slackards and talk-downers
with their minions bring us low;
those hapless politicians, too
wreak chaos (well we know).

We built our all with hand in hand
and brains and sweat and gall,
but those who don't build now demand
an equal share in all.

They'll burn all things of value down,
bring down the system, too.
With all the marble brought to ground
we'll vanish then from view.

The capitals of the world will fall;
guess it won't matter much.
We have a talent, after all,
for ruining what we touch.

Iraq Again

As my sharp wings slice cool night air,
I imagine the quietness they have tried
to paint upon themselves below me —
burnt sienna with just a smattering of
gray netting, purple and olive brush —
all indiscernible in a desert darkness,
but certain to be there all the same.

I see life stirring in a ghostly green,
leaving its refuge from the day's heat
— an ant assemblage, scurrying about.
My appendages work their cold magic,
and I circle well off to a safe distance,
eying the frantic insect encampment.
I watch it disappear in white flashes.

Just monochromatic flame flickers.
My screen cannot show me the death.
Black, acrid smoke and red of blood
are hidden away behind a green veil.
All sense of their screams and crying
is lost in my cocooned, eerie silence.
I head home, unfeeling and untouched.

A Far, Far Better Thing Not Done

you only wish the moment passed
when memory brings you 'round at last
to the point where you still had a choice
of silence or to bring to voice
that one dissent
which might have meant
another path for he who heard
who went for want of a single word
to be dead at dawn at the martyr's wall
as chaff of remorseless guillotine's fall
when you held the key
to set him free
and no objection spoken
society's bonds lay broken
and your life's worth left no token
of the better man

Freedom Dies A Little

freedom dies a little
with an unspoken word or whispered courage
an averted eye from others' wretched plight
or an ear turned deaf to cries in the night

by inches unconcerned in miles preoccupied
with creature comfort to insulate what we feel
or bald disdain hiding that less tastefully real

freedom dies a little
in first person singular when coldly self focused
from terminal hollowness if stolen or bought
or received as a gift without battles fought

in epidemics of hope someone else will stand
shed his precious blood for what's at stake
giving all he might have while others just take

freedom dies a little
from accumulating small but fateful wounds
faithfully negotiated with the best of intention
by shallow politicians seeking sure reelection

by trading off some for a bit of timed peace
or constitutional blindness for sake of security
receiving not either with any sense of surety

freedom won't die
with a storm
but with a breeze
not all at once
but piece by piece
right before our eyes

Empathy in a Desecrated Cemetery

Eerie spasms of conscience
hobnail painfully, clicking against
cobblestones in back of his eyes.
Pressing on through graves,
his throat fully heart-stuffed,
he moves mechanically, step on step
to that one harshly lamp-lit place
among scarred headstones.

He starts to scream, but is silenced
by the lockstep of boots in his ears.
This neighborhood was all Jews, then.
Now, scarcely any are left living
within the reach of a heart's caring.
He wants to scream: "It wasn't me.
I am Jewish too!" He doesn't,
because he isn't, though feels he is.

IV. Hearts Lost and Found

Teach Me Your Words

Teach me your words.
Mine flow slowly, languidly
over rolling hills and pastel colors.
Yours rush like a floodtide
over angled crags and vivid hues,
carrying off the debris and detritus
of an overly cluttered world,
leaving a clean, fresh landscape.

Teach me your words.
I am not afraid of language:
adjectives that bite and scratch,
verbs playing 'catch me if you can',
strange nouns from ethereal places.
I can see them gyrate on the page,
the odd adverb and conjunction
throwing ropes around them.

Teach me your words
so I can paint a better portrait
of worlds to be made before us.
Our thoughts dancing wildly
to the same beat, a counterpoint
harmonizing our two psyches,
synchronizing verbal vibrations
to the beauty of a single phrase.

Teach me your wonderful words.

The Night Watchman

Strands of hair lie asleep,
draped across my shoulder.
You nestle your head lightly,
in quiet seclusion from fear,
knowing well of my love
that keeps your heart safe.

I am frozen, entranced by
sleep's subtle movements
with the sound of each breath,
watching in awe as you glide
peacefully from dream to dream,
searching, I pray, for me.

Such is the time of my life —
love need not be felt by touch,
nor be voiced aloud to be heard.
It lights my very soul aglow with
a joy as bright as an internal sun.
It compels my eyes to your sleep.

Four Haiku for You

my patient soft wind
carries far more love to you
than a raging storm

the tone of my voice
tells you more of me in truth
than words of a poem

a beat from my heart
together with all its kin
is my song of love

sparks within your eyes
contain all the world I need
or ever need know

Ode to Pat Benetar

Timid loves are painfully lost
among the sharp thorns of life.
Flesh — struggled, tired and torn
— yields to the sight of blood.
Lovers shrink from the garden
as hearts, untempered by fate,
bear no toughened battle scars,
and know neither ebb nor flow
of victory on love's battlefield.

Mourning Identity

At the table's edge just beyond my reach
fingers fitfully drum a cadence of change.
I drink my coffee, and you your black tea,
while browsing obituaries in the morning paper.

You think you're me, but cannot be me,
life's turns having dealt both end and beginning.
We stare, awestruck at our eyes' reflections,
as our joys and sorrows commingle in the heart.

We pose no difference in our hopes and fears;
our characters similar, we just walk two paths.
You stand at the last and turn to take leave.
Unspoken good-byes hang ringing in the air.

You think you're me; and I? I am not at all.

Could

Could I collect
all your tears of sorrow
into one vast sea,
I would sail across it
in a skiff of hopes,
for day upon day,
making fast at long last
in the harbor of your heart.

Could I just pile
all your heavy burdens
into one high mount,
I'd climb up a ladder
of wide awake dreams
and crest trouble's peak,
making done every one
as a token of my love.

Could you see me
standing in your doorway
making true my words,
I would be yours ever
through seas of sorrow,
over mounts of trouble,
keeping love in your life
and a song upon your lips.

Betrothal

you breathe my life's worth
into whispers of your love
to tunes of white silk

Love is Creative Destruction

Love is impossible, impractical,
unpredictable, unexplainable.
It doesn't care what you think
and certainly not what you reason.

Love is at once kind and cruel,
hard and easy, clear and muddled.
Love gives, and love takes away —
but never all you have, all you need.

Love disrupts. It shakes the tree,
stands all touched lives on end,
instills anger, disbelief and hurt
along with the more normal joy.

Love is creative destruction,
demolishing one system of order
in favor of a new, often chaotic one
that roots itself in the rubble.

Fear to Love

In the depths of your heart,
where you hide me away,
where you keep me apart
from the light of the day,

I am cold and alone
in the depths of your heart,
where the doubts are your own
as they've been from the start.

Is he true, for his part,
to the love that you keep
in the depths of your heart,
where you search in your sleep?

Only when you are sure
will you see me depart,
with his love then secure
in the depths of your heart.

Choices

Life is not the same poem
written over and over again,
but an infinity of new verses
grown of one's imagination:
poems to light life's passion
to make each new dawning
a nerve tingling experience,
and not just an occurrence.

Not Just Passing Through

I am not just passing through,
over or around you.
You are not just a country station
on a branch line off the express,
where I have been diverted,
temporarily, due to track work.
I didn't have to take out a map
to find you and come to you.

You are my true destination,
not some stopping off point.
I am not vacationing, sightseeing
(though you are truly worth seeing).
I do not need glasses or contacts.
You, I know with my eyes closed.
I have my ticket. Cupid left it there
under my lonely pillow last night.

I must go now. Just a few stops
until I can discard my suitcase.

There Are Words

there are words
there are words of used to be
they climb from memory with old hands
wrinkled with the years
they are fond, were warming
some were comfortable, some painful
many were/are of old love
with rounded, mellow bass tones
echoing through the night air, for miles

there are words
there are words of sometimes
popping up at odd intervals, unpredictably
timed in their arrival
they are now and then, off and on
endearing in their periodic rediscovery
most are of likes/wants
seasoned with quaintness, sighs
feeling like a fine meal, with a good wine

there are words
there are words of maybe
wrapped in the hope of someday soon
will she, won't she
does he, doesn't he, will we
know happiness, love, contentment
words of infatuation
won't we, couldn't we, when,
boiling in a blender of hot, cold, spicy

there are words
there are words of always
safe, secure, bound up for all eternity
we are, we will be,
for us, with us, by us, just us
whatever may come, wherever we go
all words of love
everlasting, unyielding, true,
holding hands, touching, forever feeling

V. A Tour of Senses

Hay Baling

a captive of heat

shut within glass
watching a farmer's
finish to hay baling
in the summer sun

I cannot smell his
dry old mowings nor
see his glistening
sweat from afar

but sense the strain
to wring his living
from tasking land
and too long hours

his time is precious
with a cold front due
and hard rain surely
not too far behind

perhaps it'll free me

Whisperer

If I could be heard as a soft whisper
slipping through the air in tiny ripples,
my words might soothe or tempt ears
to painless reception of my thoughts.
Yet, coarse as 'croak' in a toad's voice,
my speech rides wild waves, reflecting
off ceilings and bouncing off walls.
It slices the air with malice for all quiet
and charity for no one's peace of mind.
I am, alas, an unwanted stray noise
put in my lonely place by the librarian,
cell phone barely escaped confiscation.

Dawn

How do we know the rain's song
or the homage a gentle wind
makes to earth's waking yawn?
Are we so lost in techno sounds
that we harbor no awareness
of hummingbirds batting wings
or water babbling in conversation
with the neighboring green grass?

Go out and down and away
from concrete pads and walkways,
away from glass, away from steel,
and put ear to ground and listen.
What you hear is the morning,
fresh and new, soft and warm,
arising without the works of man;
thriving, despite the works of man.

Stars

I urge the brightest stars to shine
when moon goes dark in earth eclipse
and does not overwhelm night sky
with light-filled orbital ellipse.

Within this field of colored gems
are blues and reds and other hues.
Delightful sparks so common then
I cannot bring myself to choose.

Each plays a part within my sight
and melds its twinkle with the rest —
orchestrally as spectrum light or
string quartet or jazz-like jest.

Bring forth tonight's full astral symphony
that I might relish glows from every galaxy.

In The City By The Bay

Your heart reaches for comfortable solitude
but finds only the clamor of a city at work.
Her wind-chafed skin breathes in and out
in time to the throbbing of a timeless vitality.
A hubbub of tourists and traffic steals the day
while her nights fill with the lights and scents
and sounds of a city alive, love and laughter
adrift on the air at each of a thousand corners.
She sets herself to rest only at wee hours
when streets and bay are bathed in quiet,
and nothing presumes to move in the dark
except the unfirm ground beneath your feet.

I Think I Went To Times Square Once
(For Susan)

Purple Haze inundates my ears,
dripping down granite spires to pavement
where taxis swerve and puddles reflect neon
to grab my eyes with kaleidoscope pulses.

Her tangy, pungent and piquant flavors
rise to yield a panoply of overripe aromas
in crisp night air that shivers me with energy,
my feet propelled into unfamiliar dances.

Mad celebration is her electric life force,
coursing through streets, pushing me along
to a midnight destination beyond my control.
Surrendering to inevitability, I go with the flow.

Slowly stripped of feelings, my body is afloat,
wrapped tight in a mass of teeming humanity,
one breathing organism, speaking one voice.
Awareness submerges in a collective haze.

Lightening explodes my eyes in slow motion.
An animalistic growl, born from a whisper,
drives to crescendo in a mere 10 seconds,
counted faithfully in a Babel of languages.

I am enveloped in kisses, taken and given,
as a steel guitar twangs out a new tune.
Bodies sway strangely as voices spit out
familiar words to drown in cups of kindness.

Suddenly, rock bands attack my frontal lobes,
riffing from every direction, every altitude.
I float in teeming masses again, unconscious
of time or space and lost in a oneness of all.

And then I blink awake, seemingly alone
except for whining orange street sweepers
chasing refuse of millions from my view.
She needs cleaned, for a new year's new day.

I need a shower... and some make-up sleep.

Cloud Farming

Here and there a pausing
to glimpse tiny little billows,
quick to poke their wispy heads
from furrows in the blue.
Bend and stretch for morning
ballerinas up on tip toes,
fluffy cotton candy puffs
spin sunshine in the east.

Early woke, she's watching
seedlings surf upon the thermals,
streak fair skies with slashes white,
spin whirlpools still unseen.
Clouds play hiding, seeking
within eddy currents swirling;
fingers grasping, open/ close,
in desperate search for warmth.

Standing at her window,
she can feel the air is cooling,
sensing through arthritic hands
a sudden coming change;
tracks the nimble nimbi
lines far out to the horizon;
sees it's time for harvesting
a bumper crop of rain.

Light turns into darkness
amid peals of harsh ripe thunder.
Sun takes flight in full eclipse
behind a wall of black.
Gutters fill, downspouts roar
and rain barrels overflowing,
crops of raindrops fill the barns
until the clouds are gone.

From My Kitchen Window

Soy beans dry slowly
under an unworthy sun's
September summer,
though leaves turn brown in God's time
his slow watch breeds impatience.

Dogs search the wood pile
for signs of rabbit movement,
her wind-wafted scent
betrays in hidden presence
her quest of winter nesting.

Dew laden grass leaves
shimmering in early dawn,
blind to coming mow
when all will forfeit their heads,
wave in blissful ignorance.

Pale blue autumn sky
painted across my window
fills me with comfort,
eases all angst of living,
blankets my small world like peace.

Seasonality

The all-but-barren miles of harvest
stir my soul with pangs of regret.
Mechanical memories of combines
raise metallic echoes in my ears.
I strain eyes to imagine waving grain
stretching on beyond life's horizons,
moved by wind with military precision
on an endless march to market.

This less inspiring late fall stubble,
chopped and chaffed by automatons,
arouses little passion in most poets,
save those who thrive on desolation.
Yet the call of empty rolling ground
is somehow strangely compelling
as I hand harvest words of beauty,
knowing past to be imagery of future.

Overcast

Her dreary gray skies oppress my inner spirit
and drench my pores with weariness for the day.
Windows were not made for such depressing vistas.
Rather I were left with blinds drawn closed
to enjoy the bright wanderings of my imagination.

VI. The Isle of Whimsy

Scooter The Cat

My name? Call me Scooter, the cat.
I hide in the hollow of the couch,
safe from the dog and its big black nose,
and the others in the house, I suppose.

It's lonely in the couch all alone,
but this is what I pay for my nerves —
fear and mistrust of everything around,
every bump, every move, every sound.

My humans give me treats now and then.
Okay, on their desk twice a day.
So I venture out after they are gone
eat the treats, lick my paws and move on.

And yes, I sneak out in the night
when the household as a whole is asleep;
drink fresh water at the communal bowl,
eat dry food then dash back to my hole.

Now I'll sit for some petting once awhile,
take a stroke or ten from the dad.
I tolerate enough just to make me purr,
but just move too fast and I'm a blur.

My name is still Scooter, the cat.
Seeing someone strange, I disappear.
Don't be sad if I run when you come to call,
most folks never get to see me at all.

Piano Man

My eyes float in its whorls and eddies,
ride upon its tonic scented currents
around swizzle and melting cubes,
seeking numbed Saturday night escape.
A tinkling from his piano announces
the fifth hour of my drinking since five.

I raise my sodden soul to the sounds
and feel stirred in me a vague memory.
Sad and sweet, and yet incomplete,
it drifts just beyond my recollection.
My plaintive gaze falls on Billy, nodding.
He surely must know how it goes.

So he just starts in playing the melody
that will soon have us feeling alright.
Sings us the song — he's the Piano Man.
Yes he sings us that song tonight
as I, content in my old man's clothes,
listen, making love to my tonic and gin.

Daydream in Paradise

on an island in my mind
I awake to the pitty-pat rhythm
of a small dream out in the street
making its way to morning market

its song is airy and feather light
resplendent with one day's hope
that life will be generous
and the fish fetch a fair price

the melody is my intoxication
hastening me down the stairs
and on to the pescaderia
where I want to buy all he has

i-Man

I am lost in a forest
of ratchets and gears.
Dithered by doubts,
and fractured by fears,
my confidence wanes.

As I wander so helpless
beneath touch screen sky,
endless songs loop.
Having scant idea why,
I sing the refrains.

My confusions are legion;
self-reliance is gone.
I cannot get far
with my pause button on.
What hope yet remains?

In this i-fashioned moment
a man cannot breathe.
Instantly there,
all knowledge conceived
short-circuits our brains.

Musings of an Idle Mind

Unlike prose,
with poetry one can't simply
peek at the last page
and know all the poet intended.

No matter how effusively written,
there are no words
for winning hearts
in poems left unrecited.

The poet's responsibility is
to teach, provoke or beguile,
lest words ring hollow
and shatter upon the floor.

A broken glass may be poetic metaphor.
If you glue shards into a mosaic chaos,
it's like splicing film off a cutting room floor.
What would you expect, Casablanca?

There's no synonym
for freedom.
To shade its meaning
is to hasten its loss.

A stone can never know the joy of love;
but love and joy can outlive a stone,
so long as men and women endure
and there are good poets among them.

A Slow Day At Starbucks

It's a slow day at Starbucks,
and the music is skinny vanilla
(covers of covers by wannabees).
My brain is fried by emissions
from cells in soft plush chairs.
Unengaged baristas are poised
to pounce upon any opportunity
for drink making, hot or cold.

But the machines are silent
and ice tea shakers empty.
My head aches from the droning
of some web site consultant
trying to chat up a college gal.
More polite patrons are quiet,
silently playing Words With Friends
while nursing the morning's latte.

Pictures purchased in bulk
adorn the few ad-free walls.
A balloon eclipses the sun
while the girdered Eifel tower
swings on a slim watch fob.
Bullets fly from painted houses
on burned battleground streets
in some hot Mid-Eastern city.

I wrestle futility in attempts to write
just one rhyme line, over and over.
But the day won't permit thought,
only thoughtless killing of time;
wholly lethal, unforgiving slaughter
of minutes, hours or even days.
If only I had a smart phone here,
on a slow day at Starbucks.

Weeds and Grass

There are bald spots in the lawn.
I've often nurtured grass in them,
yet develop only greater fondness
for the dandelions that grow there.
Surely nature wanted it this way,
to make our weeds grow so easily.
Grass too was part of her design —
it grows so well in my flower beds.

Oh Furtzil Sweet Amines
(A Vogon Poem)

Oh furtzil sweet amines in gobs to the glower pot.
Pray to the great Ogle for reffonimus platitudes.
For time spent flagulating revantalizes not
the spurious hoglinks of ill worn attitudes.
Urge on malodorous deponticated verse.
Stir up the pidgets of variegated grumstuff.
Melon and skither the frugal opthalogersts,
painting red curthals, balumppels just blue enough.
Morgel plith bumblers of sharp carpel tunnis,
belied by the cold, open-wallerized camp grounds,
and follow the steel grey migropes where fun is:
to the hallow pool water, where musclegird sounds.
To the hallow pool water, where gunkfish abounds,
and makes frowns, and circus rounds.

A Warrior's Tale

Cradled in attentive arms,
made safe from zombies, Nazgûl, Sith,
a slumber holds his limp form fast
in daily climb and 'cross room width.
Light saber fitted to tailored grip
never known to fall despite sleep's ease.
Legolas' bow slung snugly, mates
with a "double-tap" Colt for feisty Z's.
Now up to bed and well tucked in,
both loved and ready to abandon care,
my seven-year son turns to his right,
and says "goodnight" to his warrior bear.

Ever Been

I suppose
your day today
will be the way
your days have ever been.

Mind so numb
each break you take
you'll fight to wake
and make your day begin.

Work's so dull
your pride gets fried
so deep inside
you slide 'til work day's end.

Day's so long
you doze, pulse slows
the whistle blows
so goes your life's misspend.

Stand in place
and be not free
come seize the key
and flee the ever been.

VII. Portraits and Portrayals

Sitting on Death Row

How cold my soul in the dark
immersed in deep silent words
knowing no chance they're heard
in this place so barren, so stark.

How empty the absence of light
when hope is smothered by fear
and just retribution draws near
to blinding the stars in my night.

Oh, could my footsteps retrace
a path that takes me to black.
Alas, no choice to turn back
for consequence I must face.

How cold my soul in the dark,
in this place so barren, so stark.

Dregs Need Not Be Sour

His calloused and scarred hands,
fingernails stained of the picking,
press and preserve purple grapes.
Old gnarled vines, fallen from favor,
yield his labors a meager living
from sweet jellies sold to tourists.

I met him when wine still flowed,
aging in casks against stone walls
in cool caves under Burgundy hills.
A young man, employing townsfolk
in green vineyards and brick winery,
his vintage superb, his eyes wide.

But today this Mâconnais is aged,
dry and gnarled, much as his vines.
Life shriveled from a long drought,
he still offers me a knowing smile
and a draught of fond memories,
flooding back from better times.

We lift a glass to toast the old days,
and spread his wares on hot bread.
There are years worn upon his face,
but the caged spirit of a young man
twinkles still in his deep blue eyes
in complete absence of bitterness.

Lincoln

Who is his measure, this giant of man
who seems so much greater than you or me?
How much of him I must not understand.

Drawn deep from within, he fashioned his plan
to fight 'til they won and end slavery.
Who is his measure, this giant of man?

Father-like kindness and a blood-stained hand,
made safe the Union yet set rebels free.
How much of him I must not understand.

Yet eloquence framed his elegant stand:
bind up all our wounds, from sea to sea.
Who is his measure, this giant of man?

Then I remember he sent for the band
with the war all done, "play Dixie" his plea.
How much of him I must not understand.

For taken he was by madman's demand,
our gift not fulfilled, his work incomplete.
Who is his measure, this giant of man?
How much of him I must not understand.

Outliving

He argued with the television like an old friend,
point and counterpoint hurled at the screen,
punctuated periodically with a choice epithet
to underscore the passion of his perspective.
Yet, never was there a hint of malice intended,
for he harbored a fondness for this... device,
disagreement with whom was sustenance
for a most enduring and satisfying friendship.

One-sided as that friendship may have been,
his eyes might have closed calendars ago
were it not for its steadfast companionship,
its fueling of an otherwise stifled conversation.
Like bricks of an old house, pieces of his life
had fallen away, leaving but a fragile shell
and echoes of familiar voices within its walls.
Echoes, long since given way to silence.

So here on the battlefield of his living room
he stood his ground, as if last line of defense
against unyielding and stone-deaf arguments,
rendering blow for blow and thrust for thrust.
Often overheated, yet never ungentlemanly,
they stood at noses like two old prizefighters,
but he never once blinked, knowing the stakes.
It was the fight of his life. It was his fight for life.

50 to Life

It shreds the chapters of his life
in a twisted journey of atonement
that bleeds sorrow upon the pages,
yet leaves him only empty anguish.
He cannot unspeak hateful words,
nor undo hurtful acts of his youth,
and personal agony ends no pain
for those upon whom he visited grief.

Anointed in oils of fine self pity,
those few about him glimpse shallows
and miss the raging river of regret
that flows beneath a blistered surface.
Drowned in guilt and unforgiven
in a place devoid of any redemption,
he wears his fault like a suit of armor
and quests in the dark for exculpation.

Yet, life put away, all but forgotten,
self-punished spirit dulled of all pain,
his time stacks up in layered sheaths
that mark the years like oak tree rings.
At last mercifully achieving final days,
not free of body nor washed of hands,
he takes an ultimate loathing breath,
expecting and warranting nothing.

Oxford Literati

Our car chews up low-bid Mississippi asphalt like a last meal,
spitting out sub-one-minute miles from Memphis to Oxford,
and singing V-6 part harmony to the hum of hot bulging tires
as road patch and chuck holes beat a rhythm in our wake.

Oxford's square at noon is post-Civil War Norman Rockwell,
abuzz with coeds from Ole Miss, and OMG John Grisham
sneaking across the road and quickly hurrying on to lunch!
His furtive glances betray his fears of having been seen.

Uncertainty over it being him percolates as we hunt parking.
East Jackson yields a spot. Not thinking ourselves stalkers,
we walk to Proud Larry's eatery, ostensibly for lunch, but
following the heading last seen for our wannabee Grisham.

That angled countenance is there at the corner of the bar.
Unemulative of an old west gunslinger (back to the door),
he seems totally preoccupied with his meal, unaware of us.
We meld in with this gin mill's spate of tourists as we sit.

We argue over his authenticity, stealing occasional glances.
Penny offers a back cover book photo as her bona fides.
Younger Grisham. I proffer hair to be wrong, face too round.
I take out my camera. He stares. As I raise it, he leaves.

We came to Oxford for Faulkner, Penny's literary inamorata.
Half an hour in Square Books, and again shopping around.
Faulkner on the bench by Regions Bank — Grisham forgotten.
Rowan Oak draws Penny like trade winds to the new world.

After much circumnavigation, we find it on Old Taylor Road.
It isn't hard to understand what drove Faulkner to buy such
seclusion in the midst of southern charm to live in and write.
We buy tickets for the inevitable tour, suppressing flashes.

His house reflects all that is to be read in his many novels,
and suddenly on a wall is a large photograph of his daughter,
posed recently with Morgan Freeman and... John Grisham.
I concede to Penny, it was him! She glows all the way home.

Pompeii and Herculaneum Unearthed

It falls with the grace of stones,
fiercely shredding roof, flesh
and futile thoughts of shelter.
Face to face with nature's anger
pain is such fleeting diversion,
preoccupying the first seconds
before we yield to primal instinct
and scream our lives into night.

We are not Caesar, general
nor even high-stationed praetor
with well known family name.
Ours are the hard, coarse hands
of a bread baker, shop keeper,
vintner and amphorae bearer.
Dying here with wives and children,
we leave little for history to note.

Who may come that will know,
buried deep for many centuries
beneath their idle wanderings,
we wear the shells of our agony?
Find these echoes of humanity
so we may know peace in rest,
at last to be remembered
for the good people we were.

A Look Ahead 20 Years

The strands of my simple life
are here and there unraveled,
and gray edges peek quietly out
from a thinning mane and face.

My walk, measured with care,
is not apace with a younger gait,
but still gets me to the point
where I can use precious time.

New to the courtesies accorded
those with well-weathered walls,
I nod and thank through my day,
at seats given up and doors held.

I am unhurried in my use of years,
as each day carries on the joy
of being alive, well and in love
with she who graces my hours.

The clock ticks, wearing me away,
but the look back recounts much
that is to be savored and relished.
'ere long I go, it's been worthwhile.

Even the Dead Deserve A Song

Life's breath, losing all melody,
travels into wooden silence.
Yet the heart's enduring voice
is not prisoner to a proud past,
a once resounding epitaph
fading from one's thoughts like
a pulse that ebbs with a passing.
This loving noise rises in tune
from our full depth of memory.
We feel it harmonize with our
unbroken spirit, dispelling sights
of cold, empty coffins with a song
not of losing, but of joyously leaving
on a heavenly river, flowing to land
where to party is all that remains,
the time for sorrow having passed.

One Last Dream

Written on the walls of your life
are personal dreams, failed and bruised.
Vested in your struggle for contentment,
wounded passions leave blood stains,
dissipating into life's dark corners.
Bled out, your complexion is sickly pale.

What was it you'd most hoped for?
Was it glitter in the sunshine of youth,
or feet warming in a cold middle-age winter?
There were too many hurts to bear it all.
Coming up empty time after time; empty.
Yet here you are, and you're not done.

Hiding in your tall weeds of self doubt,
your tear-stained hand strokes the wall.
Summon strength to scratch one last dream.
All that broken nails and bloodied finger tips
can do, you do. Will it live and breathe?
You watch without time, frozen in place.

Turns come without orchestral fanfare.
They come when a piece of paper won't fit
between the giving up and the going on,
and your mind screams at you to just stop,
but your heart refuses to cease beating.
In the end, dreams are all heart, not mind.

VIII. God and Nature

Sit at the Edge of the World

Come sit with me
at the edge of the world
and stare at the nonsense
falling off and out to space.

Constructs of existence,
pillars of civilization,
all frames of reference,
float away, like so much chaff.

Things of value —
life, love, truth and beauty —
are rooted in our hearts,
remaining when all else is gone.

They are God's fine artistry.
All else is man's crass work.

He's My God Too!

She wears her symbolic faith
as an ornament of conformance,
but only to ward off trespassers
who would proselytize their own.

Many are faithful weekend warriors.
They know chapter, verse and page
but nothing of language meaning,
only that King James said so.

She speaks to Him on Tuesdays,
and six other days in the week.
I think it's using an i-Phone app,
or toll-free at 1-800-GOD-HERE.

Doesn't matter; he hears what he wants
and then puts you on hold, waiting.
The music's not bad, Blue Oyster Cult.
(He has an eclectic music collection.)

"He'll have to get back to you." Damn!
"Sorry," she says with a hint of smile.
She knows he doesn't like cursing,
just plagues, famines and floods.

Prayers from up the street, full of "please,"
"I need," "help" — analog only, not digital.
"God's, please hold. God's, please hold."
"See? Not just you," she thinks, walking by.

"Maybe he has an out-of-town gig,
or set his spam filter too high" — a thought.
She stops, looks at birds nested in a tree,
closes her eyes and leaves Him a message.

Dreams

most lives are spent
searching far horizons,
in quest of bright stars
shimmering in the night.
all are free to dream
and grasp at their own,
for God plays no favorites,
having put his stars
equally out of the reach
of everyone.

Who Are We To Blame

I wonder if God really cares.
Pain's so deep it drowns us all.
Is the flaw ingrained in our very self?
Madness, outrage, futility?

Pain's so deep it drowns us all
in the depths of our basest instincts.
Madness, outrage, futility:
chains that can only drag us down.

In the depths of our basest instincts,
floundering unrepentant of our sins —
chains that can only drag us down —
are we still redeemable in his eyes?

Floundering unrepentant of our sins,
how quick we are to forgive ourselves.
Are we still redeemable in his eyes?
If so, then perhaps we won't drown.

Sandy

Her neighbors' lives washed ashore in Amboy:
a child's toy, an empty family photo album,
a wooden piano bench (missing its top),
kitchen cabinets, bed spreads, a catcher's mitt.
That green and purple chair that perhaps sat
out at the curb in front of the Wilsons' house,
just last Friday as she happened to walk by.
Just last Friday, when she lived there.

Debris clogged lots where homes had stood,
piled with years of former precious treasures
ripped from hands and hearts by a vicious anger,
its made-for-TV devastation filling her eyes —
eyes thoroughly wet with tears of survivor's guilt.
The haunting scene of that dying roller coaster,
lapped endlessly by waves, loops in her mind
like a mobius strip, a monument to folly.

She silently walks the still sand-covered streets,
heading to the boardwalk, or where it had been.
She thinks of a hundred years of memories
washed off the face of the earth in a single day.
Her eyes catch an old man, waiting upon a boy.
Digging in rubble, the boy cries out: "here it is!"
The man's face brightens, seeing the boy's hand
clutching an undamaged painting of his grandson.

She watches the two laugh, share an embrace;
she at once understands what in life is important.
Of chairs, pianos, albums and catcher's mitts,
none matters near so much as living memories.

And God Said

Birds fly out from his cotton clouds,
piercing the gold and orange dawn
created so deftly by his artist's brush.
Greenery dripped from his palette
spawns firs and spruce to line lakes
and cover mountains to the snow line.
He gazes down from the neon rainbow,
extracting images from his sketch pad,
infusing them with all the colors of life.
At the last, a panoply of flesh tones
completes the magnificent canvas.
It hangs now by one thread of love
on the wall of his vast, black universe.

McCormick's Creek State Park

Sun flooded trees pour Jackson Pollack splotches
across roadways deep in nature's hidden heart.
Wonders of McCormick's Creek Canyon beckon,
and though Trail 3 is ominously labeled "rugged,"
trepidation gives way to foolishly re-imagined youth.

Undaunted in our descent down the canyon steps,
scant attention paid to the consequences of retreat,
the embrace of silence is broken ever-so-gently by
growing sounds of water — timeless and relentless,
gnawing its way through the miles of limestone.

With a centuries old purpose, in trickles and flood,
through brown St. Genevieve, yellow St. Louis and
finally gray/white Salem, nature's workman carved
this portrait of unspoiled beauty to greet our eyes
and test our unsteady steps upon a rough hewn path.

At once rushing, swirling, bubbling and churning
beyond boulders and forest refuse, smoothed stone
and scree fallen from collapsed steep canyon walls,
water points our way forward, glinting brightly in sun.
Our fear of needed rescue palpably fades as we walk.

Clambering up banks by grace of firmly rooted twigs,
gingerly dancing over wet rocks to cross and re-cross
the ceaseless flows of this deep, meandering gorge,
we are enveloped by a growing sense of confidence,
passing from reluctant tourists to semi-bold path finders.

Laughing proposals to scale near vertical canyon walls,
or cross the creek by blithely walking over a fallen log,
cheer our way through wide beds of jagged stones,
over tiny, precarious paths worn by previous scouts
bravely, yet vainly, in search of the illusive Trail 3.

All too soon we are at the steps leading up and out.
Our stride firm and confident now, the way clear.
Detouring from our ascent to see the falls upstream,
we revisit the power water has in shaping this world.
In this place, creating an incredible pristine beauty.

A Visit to Mound State Park

Down in the vast cathedral of trees,
gnarled and twisted in quest of sky,
the creek plays a two-part harmony
to the tunes of birds singing for supper.
Walking slopes of the ancient mounds,
crunching well-worn gravel with feet,
your pace observes the song's cadence.
In steep ravines of beaver's abandon
(their industry's debris strewn about),
gentle water eases all city burdens
for hot, tired toes of two tender lovers
trading kisses and living in the moment.

Death on the Savanna

The scent wafts across the plain,
through the trees and into the night.
Hunger rises as she senses her prey,
the sharp quarter notes of quickening pulse
pressing on her ears, deaf to all sounds
save the panicked breathing of the hunted.

Killing is natural, instinctive to the species —
a passionless act, driven only of necessity.
Death on the savanna by a hunter's moon
feeds the craving of both her and her cubs.
It is on the wind, wafting across the plain,
through the trees and into the night.

A Tanka to Buddha in the Cemetery

blank face telling not
hide your secret tears in rain
cloak wounds under leaves
speaking but to lonely wind
your silent prayer of mourning

IX. Words, Rhymes and Punctuation, Or Not

Guilty of Poetry in the 3rd Degree

Compelled to think of words that rhyme,
my conscious mind won't deign to play.
It closes down, as if to say:
the poem I write will take more time.

The floor is deep with garbage verse.
Tequila glasses line the sink,
but though my efforts really stink
attempts at rhyme could be much worse.

For heaven's sake, what rhymes with phlegm?
This poem exacts a strange revenge,
for tortured words, seeks to avenge.
For forcing rhymes, I am condemned.

Compelled to think of words that rhyme,
the poem I write will take more time.

The View From City Lights

The view from City Lights window never changes.
Over its poetry room fire escape, I can see
Mai Ling's bedding draped over her steel railing,
her son's freshly washed laundry hung upon hangers
twisted into the chaotic bundle of telephone wires
that run down her corner of the building like vines.
Two silver pigeons nest at that same frantic corner,
bringing sighs and coos to the black tar roof below,
strewn as it is with the poetry of Chinatown debris:
grocery bags and pop bottles, an inverted umbrella
lost to high winds from an embarrassed tourist's hand,
shards of glass, shreds of newspaper, pigeon crap,
and all of the other detritus of a modern city's waste.
The building's red bricks, bleached white in spots,
were piled by its layers high enough to block my view
of San Francisco's modern steel and glass skyline.
Sitting here, I am suddenly brought back to a day
before poets were entrepreneurs or book sellers,
when being in meant being all the way out, and
on the road was more than a salesman's lament,
or a Willie Nelson theme song in a cowboy bar.
What brave and free souls they all were back then.
Many sat right here. I can feel them stir my pen.

Coffee House Homage

Though thought to be strange,
his soul was printed local.
Caffeine junky boy,
found his spirit in the words;
community hero now.

Birthing a Poem

Among the many hours of night
that creep across the face of time,
those ones awake before the dawn
best suit my penning of a rhyme.

Arrived like waves upon a shore,
they leave as hushed receding tides.
If I am out when they should call
their worth just runs away and hides.

So armed am I to hog-tie phrase
and wrestle line in proper place.
Some will not fit, or make no sense.
I lock those up for 'just in case.'

Thus when sun wakes anew my day,
I have some parts, if not a whole.
In days to come I'll put and take,
until it breathes and has a soul.

Poetry Before Breakfast

Why in search of rhymes at the break of day?
Thoughts come so slowly at this morning hour.
Phrasing schemes pop up and then fade away.
Why in search of rhymes at the break of day?
Before coffee's on, what can poems say?
Feeble words run on lacking punch or power.
Why in search of rhymes at the break of day?
Thoughts come so slowly at this morning hour.

My Words at Rest

I leave my words resting in the sun,
where sharp edges can round
and overly combative verb forms
ease gently into a common tense.
Nouns lounge quietly in the tall grass
while sprightly adjectives play games,
much to the annoyance of adverbs
attempting to rest from overuse.

All require renewed strength to ready
for my imagination's next journey:
beyond similes and over metaphors,
beneath inner meaning, around rhymes,
to where winding soliloquies end
in the lovely land of timeless couplets
and verse flowing as pure and freely
as ink from the tip of this poet's pen.

Peaches and Poetry

Peaches are from Chile this time of year,
golden yellow, with deep red free stones.
But the taste isn't Georgia, or even Michigan.
I suppose they taste better home in Santiago,
where the flesh clings like poetic truth.

Words, like peaches, often don't travel well.
Written in a winter field of corn stalk stubs,
their cold, stark flavor may not be the best
when read in an alpine meadow's spring air,
or in the summer heat on a beach in Spain.

Like peaches, words can pass their prime,
their unshaven fuzz turning musty with age,
relevant to a rapidly turning world only in form.
When no longer luscious, flavor turned to dust,
their only value is as fertilizer for young seeds.

Me, I like my poetry homespun and in season,
brash and new from right around the corner,
written yesterday on the back of a napkin,
freshly stained with sundry lunch remnants.
The poets? The growers of new crops?

I prefer timid and unpeeled, forward and
puckering, hard, unripe, rough and unpolished,
inorganic, DuPont sprayed, genetically cloned,
bad tempered, ill mannered and loud voiced.
USDA certified free of any must or dust.

Special Refuge

Silence is a special refuge.
In dark corners of my mind,
where familiar thoughts lie
idle behind cobweb lace,
I bathe myself in the calm,
soothing touch and texture
of their imagined voices.

No need for speaking aloud
a word or syllable's sound
for they are as known to me
as the best of memories —
a child's laughter in Spring,
tasting fine wine at dinner,
or first looking into her eyes.

No, they come to me silently,
whispering in my mind's ear
or pictured in my mind's eye.
They're phrases of my youth,
of my growing to manhood,
learning and working, loving
and losing and loving again.

Whether by candle's flicker,
awakened from my sleep, or
amid the hustle of mid-day
scamper about work and life,
pulling at my poetic proclivity,
they force me into my refuge,
desperate for pen and paper.

Inside the Poet's Head

a poet's mania — to free his voices
plethora of restless thoughts, jostling
vying for existence upon a page
fighting for life within consciousness
before dying at younger hands

such multiple personalities disorder
compulsions to written thought
rarely sated by occasional verses
the new voices always clamor
begging to speak, to be heard

Muse

Her rhythm seeks you in the night,
at a ladder's summit, or a pool's bottom.
Unplugged and unanticipating,
you flash glimpses of laurel leaves,
channeling impulses of a brilliance
you never thought you possessed.
She electrifies your nervous system
with high voltage, but also with fear.

Press hands to temples, shoving,
cramming her back into your head
as you feel her leaking from your mind
drip by drip in tortuous forgetting.
Grasp for fragments to affix to the light
as dark diminution washes over you,
taking first her depth, then her feeling
and at the last her embodied essence.

Only vague form is left to stare at you,
out from behind fixed and dilated eyes.
You curse your missed opportunity
in words which pale before those lost.
You cling to poor, disjointed remnants,
but even these suffice to fuel wonder
as you lie awake in the night's waning;
wonder, at what might have been.

X. To Keep and Bear Arms

A Letter Found in the Trenches

I wish I could have known you,
felt the beat of your tiny heart,
marveled at your wonder-filled eyes,
been at once completely undone
by the joy in your mother's face
and disarmed by your beautiful smile.

I wish I could have held you close
in awe of the perfection of fingers,
dazzled by the wiggles of little feet,
energized by the calm of sleeping
in the face of a sad world's pain,
humbled by the purity of innocence.

I wish I could have seen you grow
into the strong son I always wanted,
or the daughter who breaks all hearts
with those sparkling eyes and dimples,
standing in the world finally at peace;
making your way with grace and dignity.

I wish I could have been a father for you,
sinfully proud of who and what you are,
as indeed, not there, I am so proud.
Purchased dearly, this will I bequeath:
a war-free world for you to live in.
It is by my blood, so steward it well.

Gettysburg in Winter

The frozen field is quiet and cold.
A crystal fog that shrouds all light,
as apparition, hangs mid-air
reflecting bloodless snowy white.

"They fought here?" asks a bundled boy.
"And died," replies an elder man.
"They died to make our country whole,
a thing you'll come to understand."

A barely sounding bugle call,
a din of muskets, canons' roar
all faintly echoed on the wind
that howls instead of sounds of war.

"Hold steady boys, don't break the line,"
a sergeant calls to boys in blue.
They fired and died upon this ground,
but would not let the rebels through.

I see the waves of gray advance
and break upon the short stone wall.
I sense them now beneath the snow,
left where they fell, left unrecalled.

For years the fields have still not healed,
nor rocks or hills been cleansed of blood.
Both time and snow have hid details
of carnage left by the deathly flood.

I stand astride old Emmetsburg road
on hot July of '63.
I brace myself against the chill,
imagining it were up to me.

Each man in blue or gray was steel;
so loved his cause, he stood and died.
Could I have grit like these today?
Stand fast to bayonets' rising tide?

These armies, not professional men,
but citizens heeding the soldier's call.
I dread that day it comes around
to me such nation's defense should fall.

So go to Gettysburg; stand in snow
and feel the pain of bloody rebirth.
You'll hear them all invest their lives.
It leaves no doubt of country's worth.

The Good Example

They would sacrifice their youth
on a ground not of their choosing,
all for lives that mattered little
to them barely months before.
Three tours in they mustered out,
chests adorned with hearts of purple;
every life they touched in country
had made theirs worth all the more.

Yet such good was not their motive
to don colors of the mountains,
nor for medals or the glory
did they take themselves to war.
They went there for an ideal
and to stand the good example
of our freedom's cost of keeping
when there's terror at the door.

I Died Tonight

I died tonight
in a fallow field,
on a hillside,
in a rice paddy.
My heart was full,
youth in bloom,
eyes to a future.
Now your memory
is the whole of me.
My past, forever,
all to be of me.
Are there children,
for the sake of me,
who walk my path?
Will they be spent
in a just cause?
Was I?

Wars Are Fought By The Sons

'Be a soldier my lad' cries the last generation.
Though you lay down your life when it's barely begun,
your traditional role is defending the nation.
Wars are brought by the fathers and fought by the sons.

All the young men went down to the town of Antietam,
where they fell by the road, early fall '62;
and the boys clad in gray who had gone up to meet 'em
are interred there as well with those boys clad in blue.

Take a walk 'midst the crosses that populate Flanders.
It is true that between them the poppies do grow.
Be they Tommies or Doughboys, Cannucks, New Zealanders,
they lay buried in Belgium so freedom we'd know.

On the beaches of Normandy there are no crosses.
All the dead there are sleeping on cliffs high above.
Boys were gone by the thousands when they tallied losses.
Many millions live free for these fine acts of love.

To Korea they came, wearing recycled gearing;
many retreads (it's said) giving war one more go.
Called obscure 'police action', a term not endearing.
Why they fought and were killed there GI's didn't know.

Talk to Vietnam vets who fought hard in Hue city;
minds were seared with the names of la Drang and Qui Nhon.
Some alive, some in Arlington; it's a damn pity
we scorned and reviled them when they came back home.

In Iraq One and Two, and Afghanistan's mountains,
there are those who bear wounds and yet others who've died.
We may build a memorial or commemorative fountain,
but this won't console all the mothers who've cried.

I do honor those soldiers who stand up to fight, but
abhorrent war cycles must come to an end.
War should be a last choice to make wrong into right, and
forever, young lives, should we be loath to spend.

'Be a soldier my lad' cries the last generation.
Though you lay down your life when it's barely begun,
your traditional role is defending the nation.
Wars are brought by the fathers and fought by the sons.

Dying With Scott In Antarctica
March 29, 1912

On an endless ghostly sea of ice,
we hold against a veil of white wind,
our tent more tomb than refuge.
Safe, but only to count final minutes,
we huddle near fire without warmth,
spared at least the fear of darkness
while last words are painfully found
in a morning's mind-numbing cold.

With bodies drained of strength and will
by this wretched beguiling wilderness,
our mastery of the pole feels but hollow.
The ash taste of Norway's flag waving,
marking zero degrees south before us,
fills our mouths still these weeks later.
Just 34 days behind Amundsen's dogs,
our bodies man-hauled near to death.

English character, so well appointed
to this noble task, defeated so cruelly,
forfeit of glory, fortune, and now life.
History will not be kind to our account
— triumph wanting, pitiful fate sealed
in an ungodly shroud of white crystals.
Perhaps a few pages for Captain Scott.
We others? — an overlooked footnote.

Howling west winds swallow voices
worn to bare whispers by exhaustion.
Dying men struggle to say good-byes
in ways men have done over centuries.
I conjure visions of Oates and Evans,
long dead on the horrible trek here.
My ink frozen, my pen slows, stops.
I think I am asleep.
Dreaming.
Gone.

Walking With Pickett

At the unsteady pace of worried men
we pare this mile across the field,
our gaze affixed to a clump of trees
wrapped tight in a ribbon of Blue.

What shell and shot did not displace
must we now move with lead and steel.
Two nations' fates held in our hands,
ours Gray if our duty's seen to.

I wrote my dear in dawn distraught
of all to come and how I feel.
I see my end, not in disgrace,
but true to what soldiers must do.

The cup of tears I spent may ne'er
afford her any grief repealed.
A letter is but a lover's knot
from hell in a wartime adieu.

Now soldier on with swallowed fears
in 'danse macabre,' parade surreal,
with eyes set firm to country's care,
in hope God lets me come through.

But if we share the great beyond
or other parts not so ideal,
I'll raise my cup in brethren cheers,
you Gray or the wearer of Blue.

I don't know where or when the war
will find an end and wounds be healed,
but you and I will be long gone
to legend once yearly renewed.

On Cemetery Ridge

A silent shade of black
brings night to the field.
Fear burns like hot steel
quenched in cold sweat.
Water inhaled in gulps
exhales a clammy vapor,
shrouding my young face
from a torch light's glow.

I am not dead tonight,
but tonight isn't tomorrow,
so last notes are sounded
upon paper in darkness.
Dawn is in God's hands.
I hold hope down inside,
but know it's early rising
may be suddenly lethal.

This is the final breaking
of morning and men.
Joints ache in the cold,
though it is early July.
I take a last sip of coffee,
a last glance about me,
a last gasp of living
before holding the line.

Standing in the WWII Memorial

Most all are fallen of the struggle,
bodies broken, hills long climbed.
Bloodied footprints, now illusions,
traces wiped by wind and time.

Most all inscribed, cut into marble,
deeds depicted not well known;
sacrifices undervalued,
ticker tape long swept or blown.

Most all too humble, quiet spoken;
unpretentious, valor's few.
Thanked too little for their duty,
nation's debt too long ignored.

Most all are fallen. Take their notice.
We won't see their like again.
They ask nothing save our caring;
take some time to honor them.

Dying on Corregidor

Come kiss me soft princess,
for I am unused to tenderness,
and life about me is broken
into small, jagged pieces.
They make my hands to bleed,
and defy my reassembly.

I've died a thousand times,
all in the agony of my mind's eye.
Here with you, I die painlessly,
afloat on a lamabanog sea.
Your smock comingles mine
with the blood of so many.

This rock, left barren and burnt
is fitting enough tombstone for us.
It awaits only carved inscription,
when sanity shall be restored:
"What we could, with what we had."
No one could have asked more.

Brief Biographies

Frederick Michaels lives in retirement at his home in Indianapolis, Indiana. In addition to prompting by his wonderful wife and grown children, myriad friends and acquaintances, three hyper dogs and one lonely cat, he draws his poetic inspiration from the beautiful intricacy of the English language and the vast bandwidth of information with which existence inundates his senses. His poetry has appeared in *Flying Island, So It Goes Literary Journal, The Boston Poetry Journal, Branches Magazine* and *Lone Stars Magazine*, among others. His work has also appeared in several poetry anthologies. *Potholes In The Universe* is his first book of collected poems.

Though an engineer by training, Michaels has always been pulled to the side of the arts by his love for words. He particularly enjoys the challenge poets have to convey both texture and meaning using words, without succumbing to maudlin, ugly or overly ebullient emotions. He would say that the words are always there. They just need to be properly chosen, then put in the proper order.

Taran Lopez is a sci-fi and fantasy-obsessed illustrator, animator and designer with a love of the unusual, a penchant for pop culture mashups and a specialty in comic and cartoon drawing. Her work has appeared as infographics, emojis, ecards, apparel, video games and more. She particularly loves drawing fantasy creatures, weaponry and maps. In addition to the cover of "Potholes in the Universe," she drew and designed the cover for the horror novel "Anthorrorgy" and has illustrated two children's books – *Etienne and the Starlight Express* and *Fish Wants to Fly*. She earned her B.F.A. in Illustration and Animation from Parsons School of Design in New York. When she isn't creating, Taran enjoys traveling, visiting spas, marathoning TV series, collecting ridiculous amounts of Funko Pop minis and participating in live action and tabletop role-playing games. She lives in Brooklyn, NY with her wife. More of her artwork can be found at TaranLopez.com.

Robin A. Rothman is an unapologetic grammar fascist who can spot a typo a mile away and will fight to the death against the Oxford comma. From MTV to Amazon Books, she's edited across entertainment and beyond. As a writer, she's been a lammy-slinging music journalist, a remote-wielding TV beat critic and a margin-marking book reviewer. Her byline has appeared in the Village Voice, Time Out New York, AOL, CMJ, RollingStone.com and more. She holds a Masters degree in Journalism from NYU. When she's not working with words, she is known to indulge in voracious reading binges, instigate puddle-jumping battles, embark on spontaneous adventures, partake in rapt people watching and impulsively start new craft and cooking projects. She lives in Brooklyn, NY with her wife.

www.ingramcontent.com/pod-product-compliance
Lightning Source LLC
Chambersburg PA
CBHW060353090426
42734CB00011B/2128